Productivity grows best in the soil of consistency.

SAM PENNY
The Topify Method

topifymethod.com

Chips Investments Pty Ltd
Parcel Collect 10042 76215
Shop 4, 44 Landsborough Parade
Golden Beach QLD 4551 Australia

Chips
Investments
AUST

Chips Investments Pty Ltd is the publisher of this book. More information can be found at www.topifymethod.com.

Copyright © Sam Penny 2025

All rights reserved. No part of this book may be reproduced, stored in a retrieval system, or transmitted in any form or by any means—electronic, mechanical, photocopying, recording, or otherwise—without prior written permission from the publisher, except for brief quotations used in a review or critical analysis.

A CIP catalogue record for this book is available from the National Library of Australia.
ISBN 978-1-7638968-1-9

Design by Sam Penny

Chips Investments Pty Ltd is committed to sustainability. This book is printed on paper sourced from responsibly managed forests.

DEDICATION

For all those striving to be better than yesterday.
Your next step is an adventure.

How to Use The Topify Method

Welcome to The Topify Method, your simple and effective tool for staying focused and making progress every day. This journal is designed for everyone—mums, business owners, travellers, artists—anyone looking to make the most of their time and achieve more.

At the heart of this planner is The Topify Method—a simple yet powerful system to help you align your daily actions with your bigger goals. Each Quarter, Month, Week, and Day, you'll write down your Top 5 priorities and focus on completing at least the Top 1. Small steps, taken consistently, lead to big results.

Celebrate each achievement!

SCAN TO
LEARN
MORE

How to Achieve More

Quarterly Focus
Write down your Top 3 Priorities for the next three months. These will guide your monthly and weekly plans to ensure every step moves you forward.

Monthly Focus
From your quarterly goals, choose the Top 5 things to accomplish this month. Keep it clear and actionable.

Weekly Focus
Break your monthly goals into smaller actions. Write down the Top 5 tasks for the week and focus on making progress.

Daily Focus
Each day, list your Top 5 tasks and commit to completing at least the Top 1. Progress comes from action.

Reflection & Looking Ahead
Take a moment at the end of each period—whether it's a day, week, month, or quarter—to reflect on your progress. What worked well? What challenges did you overcome? Celebrate your achievements, no matter how small. Then, look ahead—what's the next step to keep moving forward?

This planner is here to simplify your productivity, keep you focused, and help you achieve more—one step at a time. Let's make every day count!

SCAN TO LEARN MORE

Quarter: _____ to _____

My 3 Big Priorities This Quarter

Priority 1:

_____
_____

Priority 2:

_____
_____

Priority 3:

_____
_____

Why these 3?

Priority 1:

_____
_____

Priority 2:

_____
_____

Priority 3:

_____
_____

What Does Success Look Like?

Priority 1: _____

Priority 2: _____

Priority 3: _____

My Top 5 for Alignment

Main Focus: _____
Consistent Action: _____
Quick Wins: _____
_____
_____
Biggest Challenge: _____
One Rule to Follow: _____

Quarterly Commitment Statement

I commit to _____ over the next 90 days because _____
_____
_____

Month: _____

My Top 5 for this Month

Top 1 Done

○ ☐ _____

○ ☐ _____

○ ☐ _____

○ ☐ _____

○ ☐ _____

Are these aligned with my Quarterly Top 5?

Energy flows, where focus goes.

Week Starting: _____ (2)

My Top 5 for this Week

Top 1 Done

○ ☐ _____

○ ☐ _____

○ ☐ _____

○ ☐ _____

○ ☐ _____

Are these aligned with my Monthly Top 5?

Your future self is watching - go!

My top 5 for today

Top 1   Done

○ ☐ _____

○ ☐ _____

○ ☐ _____

○ ☐ _____

○ ☐ _____

Are these aligned with my Weekly Top 5?

You'll never finish if you never begin—
progress is the only way.

Date: _____ Day: _____   ①

My top win today was:

Today I am grateful for:

My top 5 for today

Top 1 Done

○ ☐ _____

○ ☐ _____

○ ☐ _____

○ ☐ _____

○ ☐ _____

Are these aligned with my Weekly Top 5?

Strip away the trivial; highlight what really counts.

Date: _____   Day: _____   (2)

My top win today was:

Today I am grateful for:

My top 5 for today

Top 1 Done

○ ☐ _____

○ ☐ _____

○ ☐ _____

○ ☐ _____

○ ☐ _____

Are these aligned with my Weekly Top 5?

Procrastination is just yesterday's self-doubt repeated—break the cycle.

Date: _____ Day: _____   (3)

_____
_____
_____
_____
_____
_____
_____
_____
_____
_____
_____
_____
_____
_____
_____
_____
_____
_____
_____
_____
_____
_____

My top win today was: _____

Today I am grateful for: _____

My top 5 for today

Top 1 Done

○ ☐ _____

○ ☐ _____

○ ☐ _____

○ ☐ _____

○ ☐ _____

Are these aligned with my Weekly Top 5?

Honor the progress
that only you can see.

Date: _____ Day: _____ (4)

My top win today was: _____

Today I am grateful for: _____

My top 5 for today

Top 1 Done

○ ☐ _____

○ ☐ _____

○ ☐ _____

○ ☐ _____

○ ☐ _____

Are these aligned with my Weekly Top 5?

Stop planning the perfect time; make this moment perfect instead.

Date: _____ Day: _____ (5)

My top win today was: _____

Today I am grateful for: _____

My top 5 for today

Top 1 Done

○ ☐ _____

○ ☐ _____

○ ☐ _____

○ ☐ _____

○ ☐ _____

Are these aligned with my Weekly Top 5?

Your future stands on the shoulders of
what you do in this very moment.

Date: _____ Day: _____ (6)

My top win today was:

Today I am grateful for:

My top 5 for today

Top 1 Done

○ □ _____

○ □ _____

○ □ _____

○ □ _____

○ □ _____

Are these aligned with my Weekly Top 5?

Let progress handle your journey;
perfection can't even start it.

Date: _____ Day: _____ (7)

My top win today was: _____

Today I am grateful for: _____

Week Ending: _____   (1)

My Week in Review

My top win this week was:
_____
_____
_____

I am grateful for:
_____
_____
_____

What could be improved or learned:
_____
_____
_____

Week Starting: _____   (2)

My Top 5 for this Week

Top 1 Done
○ ☐ _____

○ ☐ _____

○ ☐ _____

○ ☐ _____

○ ☐ _____

Are these aligned with my Monthly Top 5?

Done is better than perfect.

My top 5 for today

Top 1 Done

○ ☐ _____

○ ☐ _____

○ ☐ _____

○ ☐ _____

○ ☐ _____

Are these aligned with my Weekly Top 5?

Simplicity is the quickest route to genuine productivity.

Date: _____   Day: _____   (8)

_____
_____
_____
_____
_____
_____
_____
_____
_____
_____
_____
_____
_____
_____
_____
_____
_____
_____
_____
_____

My top win today was: _____

Today I am grateful for: _____

My top 5 for today

Top 1   Done

○ ☐ _____

○ ☐ _____

○ ☐ _____

○ ☐ _____

○ ☐ _____

Are these aligned with my Weekly Top 5?

No one's losing sleep over your struggles
—so step up and fight for yourself.

Date: _____   Day: _____   (9)

My top win today was:

Today I am grateful for:

My top 5 for today

Top 1 Done

○ ☐ _____

○ ☐ _____

○ ☐ _____

○ ☐ _____

○ ☐ _____

Are these aligned with my Weekly Top 5?

Align your actions with your aspirations.

Date: _____   Day: _____   (10)

My top win today was: _____

Today I am grateful for: _____

My top 5 for today

Top 1 Done

○ ☐ _____

○ ☐ _____

○ ☐ _____

○ ☐ _____

○ ☐ _____

Are these aligned with my Weekly Top 5?

Start with a rough draft; perfection would leave the page blank.

Date: _____ Day: _____ (11)

My top win today was:

Today I am grateful for:

My top 5 for today

Top 1 Done

○ ☐ _____

○ ☐ _____

○ ☐ _____

○ ☐ _____

○ ☐ _____

Are these aligned with my Weekly Top 5?

Aim to shock yourself with how much you can accomplish today.

Date: _____ Day: _____ (12)

My top win today was: _____

Today I am grateful for: _____

My top 5 for today

Top 1   Done

○ ☐ _____

○ ☐ _____

○ ☐ _____

○ ☐ _____

○ ☐ _____

Are these aligned with my Weekly Top 5?

You're not stuck; you're simply one
action away from progress.

Date: _____ Day: _____ (13)

My top win today was: _____

Today I am grateful for: _____

My top 5 for today

Top 1 Done
○ ☐ _____

○ ☐ _____

○ ☐ _____

○ ☐ _____

○ ☐ _____

Are these aligned with my Weekly Top 5?

Start uncertain; finish unstoppable.

Date: _____ Day: _____ (14)

My top win today was:

Today I am grateful for:

Week Ending: _____

My Week in Review

My top win this week was:

_____
_____
_____

I am grateful for:

_____
_____
_____

What could be improved or learned:

_____
_____
_____

Week Starting: _____ (3)

My Top 5 for this Week

Top 1 Done

○ ☐ _____

○ ☐ _____

○ ☐ _____

○ ☐ _____

○ ☐ _____

Are these aligned with my Monthly Top 5?

Small steps, big results.

My top 5 for today

Top 1 Done

○ ☐ _____

○ ☐ _____

○ ☐ _____

○ ☐ _____

○ ☐ _____

Are these aligned with my Weekly Top 5?

Honoring yourself is the first step
toward inspiring others.

Date: _____ Day: _____ (15)

My top win today was:

Today I am grateful for:

My top 5 for today

Top 1   Done

○ ☐ ....

○ ☐ ....

○ ☐ ....

○ ☐ ....

○ ☐ ....

Are these aligned with my Weekly Top 5?

Align your actions with what you truly
value, then watch your life align too.

Date: _____ Day: _____ (16)

My top win today was: _____

Today I am grateful for: _____

My top 5 for today

Top 1 Done

○ ☐ _____

○ ☐ _____

○ ☐ _____

○ ☐ _____

○ ☐ _____

Are these aligned with my Weekly Top 5?

Simplify your focus to amplify your results.

Date: _____ Day: _____ (17)

My top win today was: _____

Today I am grateful for: _____

My top 5 for today

Top 1 Done

○ ☐ _____

○ ☐ _____

○ ☐ _____

○ ☐ _____

○ ☐ _____

Are these aligned with my Weekly Top 5?

Your best self emerges when you're grateful
for who you are and where you stand.

Date: _____ Day: _____ (18)

My top win today was:

Today I am grateful for:

My top 5 for today

Top 1 Done

○ ☐ _____

○ ☐ _____

○ ☐ _____

○ ☐ _____

○ ☐ _____

Are these aligned with my Weekly Top 5?

Aim for progress more than perfection—
progress keeps you moving.

Date: _____   Day: _____   (19)

My top win today was: _____

Today I am grateful for: _____

My top 5 for today

Top 1 Done

◯ ☐ _____

◯ ☐ _____

◯ ☐ _____

◯ ☐ _____

◯ ☐ _____

Are these aligned with my Weekly Top 5?

Simplify your path to magnify your impact.

Date: _____ Day: _____ (20)

My top win today was:

Today I am grateful for:

My top 5 for today

Top 1 Done
○ ☐ _____

○ ☐ _____

○ ☐ _____

○ ☐ _____

○ ☐ _____

Are these aligned with my Weekly Top 5?

Start loving yourself fiercely; it's the ultimate revolution.

Date: _____ Day: _____ (21)

My top win today was: _____

Today I am grateful for: _____

Week Ending: _____

My Week in Review

My top win this week was:

_____
_____
_____

I am grateful for:

_____
_____
_____

What could be improved or learned:

_____
_____
_____

Week Starting: _____ (4)

My Top 5 for this Week

Top 1 Done

○ ☐ _____

○ ☐ _____

○ ☐ _____

○ ☐ _____

○ ☐ _____

Are these aligned with my Monthly Top 5?

One task. Full focus. Crush it.

My top 5 for today

Top 1   Done

○ ☐ _____

○ ☐ _____

○ ☐ _____

○ ☐ _____

○ ☐ _____

Are these aligned with my Weekly Top 5?

Your bed is cozy, but your goals need you more.

Date: _____ Day: _____ (22)

My top win today was:

Today I am grateful for:

My top 5 for today

Top 1 Done

○ ☐ _____

○ ☐ _____

○ ☐ _____

○ ☐ _____

○ ☐ _____

Are these aligned with my Weekly Top 5?

Simplify your tasks to magnify your impact.

Date: _____   Day: _____   (23)

_____
_____
_____
_____
_____
_____
_____
_____
_____
_____
_____
_____
_____
_____
_____
_____
_____
_____
_____
_____

My top win today was: _____

Today I am grateful for: _____

My top 5 for today

Top 1 Done

○ ☐ ....

○ ☐ ....

○ ☐ ....

○ ☐ ....

○ ☐ ....

Are these aligned with my Weekly Top 5?

Your calendar reflects your
commitments—choose them wisely.

Date: _____ Day: _____ (24)

My top win today was:

Today I am grateful for:

My top 5 for today

Top 1 Done

○ ☐ _____

○ ☐ _____

○ ☐ _____

○ ☐ _____

○ ☐ _____

Are these aligned with my Weekly Top 5?

Let your actions today echo in the success of your tomorrow.

Date: _____ Day: _____ (25)

My top win today was:

Today I am grateful for:

My top 5 for today

Top 1 Done

○ ☐ _____

○ ☐ _____

○ ☐ _____

○ ☐ _____

○ ☐ _____

Are these aligned with my Weekly Top 5?

Small strides daily can move mountains over time.

Date: _____   Day: _____   (26)

My top win today was: _____

Today I am grateful for: _____

My top 5 for today

Top 1   Done

○ ☐ _____

○ ☐ _____

○ ☐ _____

○ ☐ _____

○ ☐ _____

Are these aligned with my Weekly Top 5?

When you conquer this moment, you carve the path for your future.

Date: _____ Day: _____ (27)

My top win today was: _____

Today I am grateful for: _____

My top 5 for today

Top 1 Done

○ ☐ _____

○ ☐ _____

○ ☐ _____

○ ☐ _____

○ ☐ _____

Are these aligned with my Weekly Top 5?

Watch how far you can go when you stop looking for a push from others.

Date: _____ Day: _____ (28)

My top win today was:

Today I am grateful for:

Week Ending: _____

④

My Week in Review

My top win this week was:
_____
_____

I am grateful for:
_____
_____

What could be improved or learned:
_____
_____

Week Starting: _____ ⑤

My Top 5 for this Week

Top 1 Done

○ ☐ _____

○ ☐ _____

○ ☐ _____

○ ☐ _____

○ ☐ _____

Are these aligned with my Monthly Top 5?

Win the day, every day.

My top 5 for today

Top 1 Done
○ ☐ _____

○ ☐ _____

○ ☐ _____

○ ☐ _____

○ ☐ _____

Are these aligned with my Weekly Top 5?

Small, bold steps lead to mighty outcomes.

Date: _____ Day: _____ (29)

_____
_____
_____
_____
_____
_____
_____
_____
_____
_____
_____
_____
_____
_____
_____
_____
_____
_____
_____
_____
_____
_____

My top win today was: _____
_____

Today I am grateful for: _____

My top 5 for today

Top 1 Done

○ ☐ _____

○ ☐ _____

○ ☐ _____

○ ☐ _____

○ ☐ _____

Are these aligned with my Weekly Top 5?

Their opinions of you don't carry the weight of your self-worth.

Date: _____ Day: _____   (30)

My top win today was: _____

Today I am grateful for: _____

My top 5 for today

Top 1   Done

○ ☐ _____

○ ☐ _____

○ ☐ _____

○ ☐ _____

○ ☐ _____

Are these aligned with my Weekly Top 5?

Time rewards consistent seeds of effort
with a harvest of success.

Date: _____ Day: _____   (31)

My top win today was: _____

Today I am grateful for: _____

Month: _____

My Month in Review

My top win last month was:

_____
_____

I am grateful for:

_____
_____

What could be improved or learned:

_____
_____

Month: _____ (2)

My Top 5 for this Month

Top 1 Done

○ ☐ _____

○ ☐ _____

○ ☐ _____

○ ☐ _____

○ ☐ _____

Are these aligned with my Quarterly Top 5?

Less thinking, more doing.

Week Ending: _____

My Week in Review

My top win this week was:

_____
_____

I am grateful for:

_____
_____

What could be improved or learned:

_____
_____

Week Starting: _____

(6)

My Top 5 for this Week

Top 1 Done

○ ☐ _____

○ ☐ _____

○ ☐ _____

○ ☐ _____

○ ☐ _____

Are these aligned with my Monthly Top 5?

Success loves speed.

My top 5 for today

Top 1　Done
○ ☐ _____

○ ☐ _____

○ ☐ _____

○ ☐ _____

○ ☐ _____

Are these aligned with my Weekly Top 5?

Snap out of sleep mode; the world needs your energy.

Date: _____ Day: _____ (1)

My top win today was: _____

Today I am grateful for: _____

My top 5 for today

Top 1   Done

○ □ _____

○ □ _____

○ □ _____

○ □ _____

○ □ _____

Are these aligned with my Weekly Top 5?

Stand for yourself when it feels like you stand alone—strength is forged in solitude.

Date: _____ Day: _____ ②

My top win today was: _____

Today I am grateful for: _____

My top 5 for today

Top 1   Done

○ ☐ _____

○ ☐ _____

○ ☐ _____

○ ☐ _____

○ ☐ _____

Are these aligned with my Weekly Top 5?

Choose progress over procrastination, every time.

Date: _____ Day: _____   (3)

My top win today was:

Today I am grateful for:

My top 5 for today

Top 1 Done

○ ☐ _____

○ ☐ _____

○ ☐ _____

○ ☐ _____

○ ☐ _____

Are these aligned with my Weekly Top 5?

Sometimes the boldest move
is just to begin.

Date: _____   Day: _____   (4)

My top win today was: _____

Today I am grateful for: _____

My top 5 for today

Top 1　Done

○ ☐ _____

○ ☐ _____

○ ☐ _____

○ ☐ _____

○ ☐ _____

Are these aligned with my Weekly Top 5?

When you give your all to now, you give your best self to tomorrow.

Date: _____ Day: _____ (5)

My top win today was:

Today I am grateful for:

My top 5 for today

Top 1 Done

○ ☐ _____

○ ☐ _____

○ ☐ _____

○ ☐ _____

○ ☐ _____

Are these aligned with my Weekly Top 5?

Perfection traps you in thought;
progress frees you to act.

Date: _____   Day: _____   (6)

My top win today was:

Today I am grateful for:

My top 5 for today

Top 1 Done

○ ☐ _____

○ ☐ _____

○ ☐ _____

○ ☐ _____

○ ☐ _____

Are these aligned with my Weekly Top 5?

Sometimes the bravest thing is to keep going—do it anyway.

Date: _____ Day: _____   (7)

My top win today was: _____

Today I am grateful for: _____

Week Ending: _____

My Week in Review

My top win this week was:

_____
_____
_____

I am grateful for:

_____
_____
_____

What could be improved or learned:

_____
_____
_____

Week Starting: _____   (7)

My Top 5 for this Week

Top 1 Done
○ ☐ _____

○ ☐ _____

○ ☐ _____

○ ☐ _____

○ ☐ _____

Are these aligned with my Monthly Top 5?

Action beats intention - start now, refine later.

My top 5 for today

Top 1 Done

○ ☐ _____

○ ☐ _____

○ ☐ _____

○ ☐ _____

○ ☐ _____

Are these aligned with my Weekly Top 5?

No one owes you their care, so owe it to yourself to press on.

Date: _____   Day: _____   (8)

My top win today was:

Today I am grateful for:

My top 5 for today

Top 1 Done

○ ☐ _____

○ ☐ _____

○ ☐ _____

○ ☐ _____

○ ☐ _____

Are these aligned with my Weekly Top 5?

Fail quickly, learn rapidly,
progress steadily.

Date: _____   Day: _____   (9)

_____
_____
_____
_____
_____
_____
_____
_____
_____
_____
_____
_____
_____
_____
_____
_____
_____
_____
_____
_____
_____
_____
_____

My top win today was: _____

Today I am grateful for: _____

My top 5 for today

Top 1   Done

○ ☐ _____

○ ☐ _____

○ ☐ _____

○ ☐ _____

○ ☐ _____

Are these aligned with my Weekly Top 5?

Start where you are; perfection is just a polished delay.

Date: _____ Day: _____ (10)

My top win today was:

Today I am grateful for:

My top 5 for today

Top 1   Done

○ ☐ _____

○ ☐ _____

○ ☐ _____

○ ☐ _____

○ ☐ _____

Are these aligned with my Weekly Top 5?

Chase your happiness, and your future self will thank you.

Date: _____ Day: _____ (11)

My top win today was: _____

Today I am grateful for: _____

My top 5 for today

Top 1 Done

○ ☐ _____

○ ☐ _____

○ ☐ _____

○ ☐ _____

○ ☐ _____

Are these aligned with my Weekly Top 5?

Fail gracefully; it's one more stepping stone to success.

Date: _____ Day: _____ (12)

My top win today was: _____

Today I am grateful for: _____

My top 5 for today

Top 1   Done

○ ☐ _____

○ ☐ _____

○ ☐ _____

○ ☐ _____

○ ☐ _____

Are these aligned with my Weekly Top 5?

Spark your own flame of self-belief, and watch how it illuminates your world.

Date: _____ Day: _____ (13)

My top win today was:

Today I am grateful for:

My top 5 for today

Top 1 Done

○ ☐ _____

○ ☐ _____

○ ☐ _____

○ ☐ _____

○ ☐ _____

Are these aligned with my Weekly Top 5?

Small steps toward self-love lead to grand transformations.

Date: _____ Day: _____ (14)

My top win today was: _____

Today I am grateful for: _____

Week Ending: _____

My Week in Review

My top win this week was:

_____
_____

I am grateful for:

_____
_____

What could be improved or learned:

_____
_____
_____

Week Starting: _____   (8)

My Top 5 for this Week

Top 1 Done

○ ☐ _____

○ ☐ _____

○ ☐ _____

○ ☐ _____

○ ☐ _____

Are these aligned with my Monthly Top 5?

Progress > Perfection - Just Start

My top 5 for today

Top 1 Done

○ ☐ _____

○ ☐ _____

○ ☐ _____

○ ☐ _____

○ ☐ _____

Are these aligned with my Weekly Top 5?

Done is better than perfect—make progress and refine later.

Date: _____ Day: _____ (15)

My top win today was:

Today I am grateful for:

My top 5 for today

Top 1   Done

○ ☐ _____

○ ☐ _____

○ ☐ _____

○ ☐ _____

○ ☐ _____

Are these aligned with my Weekly Top 5?

Speech is cheap, but consistent steps accumulate priceless results.

Date: _____   Day: _____   (16)

My top win today was:

Today I am grateful for:

My top 5 for today

Top 1   Done

○ ☐ _____

○ ☐ _____

○ ☐ _____

○ ☐ _____

○ ☐ _____

Are these aligned with my Weekly Top 5?

If no one cares, let the quiet be your invitation to outdo your own past.

Date: _____ Day: _____ (17)

My top win today was: _____

Today I am grateful for: _____

My top 5 for today

Top 1 Done

○ ☐ _____

○ ☐ _____

○ ☐ _____

○ ☐ _____

○ ☐ _____

Are these aligned with my Weekly Top 5?

Dream boldly, work steadily, achieve consistently.

Date: _____ Day: _____ (18)

My top win today was: _____

Today I am grateful for: _____

My top 5 for today

Top 1   Done

○ ☐ _____

○ ☐ _____

○ ☐ _____

○ ☐ _____

○ ☐ _____

Are these aligned with my Weekly Top 5?

Spend your days on what drives you, not just what fills the hours.

Date: _____ Day: _____ (19)

My top win today was: _____

Today I am grateful for: _____

My top 5 for today

Top 1 Done
○ ☐ _____

○ ☐ _____

○ ☐ _____

○ ☐ _____

○ ☐ _____

Are these aligned with my Weekly Top 5?

Sometimes loneliness is the wake-up call you need to rebuild yourself.

Date: _____ Day: _____ (20)

My top win today was: _____

Today I am grateful for: _____

My top 5 for today

Top 1　Done

○ ☐ _____

○ ☐ _____

○ ☐ _____

○ ☐ _____

○ ☐ _____

Are these aligned with my Weekly Top 5?

Small actions done daily
create massive impact.

Date: _____   Day: _____   21

My top win today was: _____

Today I am grateful for: _____

Week Ending: _____

My Week in Review

My top win this week was:

_____
_____
_____

I am grateful for:

_____
_____
_____

What could be improved or learned:

_____
_____
_____

Week Starting: _____

My Top 5 for this Week

Top 1 Done

○ ☐ _____

○ ☐ _____

○ ☐ _____

○ ☐ _____

○ ☐ _____

Are these aligned with my Monthly Top 5?

Progress beats perfection.
Take one step forward this week.

My top 5 for today

Top 1   Done

○ ☐ _____

○ ☐ _____

○ ☐ _____

○ ☐ _____

○ ☐ _____

Are these aligned with my Weekly Top 5?

Stand in your power, even if the crowd refuses to see the stage.

Date: _____ Day: _____ (22)

My top win today was: _____

Today I am grateful for: _____

My top 5 for today

Top 1 Done

○ ☐ _____

○ ☐ _____

○ ☐ _____

○ ☐ _____

○ ☐ _____

Are these aligned with my Weekly Top 5?

Dare to succeed before letting fear plan your future.

Date: _____ Day: _____ (23)

My top win today was: _____

Today I am grateful for: _____

My top 5 for today

Top 1   Done

○ ☐ _____

○ ☐ _____

○ ☐ _____

○ ☐ _____

○ ☐ _____

Are these aligned with my Weekly Top 5?

Perfection starves your potential;
progress feeds your dreams.

Date: _____ Day: _____ (24)

My top win today was:

Today I am grateful for:

My top 5 for today

Top 1 Done

○ ☐ _____

○ ☐ _____

○ ☐ _____

○ ☐ _____

○ ☐ _____

Are these aligned with my Weekly Top 5?

Stand tall because your dreams matter,
even if no one else sees them yet.

Date: _____ Day: _____ (25)

My top win today was:

Today I am grateful for:

My top 5 for today

Top 1 Done

○ ☐ _____

○ ☐ _____

○ ☐ _____

○ ☐ _____

○ ☐ _____

Are these aligned with my Weekly Top 5?

Kindness toward yourself fuels kindness for the world.

Date: _____ Day: _____ (26)

My top win today was:

Today I am grateful for:

My top 5 for today

Top 1 Done

○ ☐ _____

○ ☐ _____

○ ☐ _____

○ ☐ _____

○ ☐ _____

Are these aligned with my Weekly Top 5?

Small actions done consistently build monumental outcomes.

Date: _____ Day: _____ (27)

My top win today was: _____

Today I am grateful for: _____

My top 5 for today

Top 1 Done

○ ☐ _____

○ ☐ _____

○ ☐ _____

○ ☐ _____

○ ☐ _____

Are these aligned with my Weekly Top 5?

Stand tall in gratitude—your posture of thankfulness elevates everything.

Date: _____ Day: _____ (28)

My top win today was: _____

Today I am grateful for: _____

Week Ending: _____

My Week in Review

My top win this week was:
_____
_____
_____

I am grateful for:
_____
_____
_____

What could be improved or learned:
_____
_____
_____

Week Starting: _____ (10)

My Top 5 for this Week

Top 1 Done

○ ☐ _____

○ ☐ _____

○ ☐ _____

○ ☐ _____

○ ☐ _____

Are these aligned with my Monthly Top 5?

Perfection is a thief. Progress is the real prize.

My top 5 for today

Top 1 Done

○ ☐ _____

○ ☐ _____

○ ☐ _____

○ ☐ _____

○ ☐ _____

Are these aligned with my Weekly Top 5?

Sow intention in the present, reap greatness in the future.

Date: _____ Day: _____ 29

My top win today was: _____

Today I am grateful for: _____

My top 5 for today

Top 1 Done

○ ☐ _____

○ ☐ _____

○ ☐ _____

○ ☐ _____

○ ☐ _____

Are these aligned with my Weekly Top 5?

Sink into the now—real change doesn't happen in theory, but in action.

Date: _____ Day: _____   (30)

My top win today was: _____

Today I am grateful for: _____

My top 5 for today

Top 1 Done
○ ☐ ....

○ ☐ ....

○ ☐ ....

○ ☐ ....

○ ☐ ....

Are these aligned with my Weekly Top 5?

Start acting; your energy will follow.

Date: _____   Day: _____   (31)

My top win today was: _____

Today I am grateful for: _____

Month: _____

My Month in Review

My top win last month was:

_____
_____
_____

I am grateful for:

_____
_____
_____

What could be improved or learned:

_____
_____
_____

Month: _____

My Top 5 for this Month

Top 1 Done

○ □ _____

○ □ _____

○ □ _____

○ □ _____

○ □ _____

Are these aligned with my Quarterly Top 5?

*Chasing perfection steals your time—
progress pays the real rewards.*

Week Ending: _____

My Week in Review

My top win this week was:

_____
_____
_____

I am grateful for:

_____
_____
_____

What could be improved or learned:

_____
_____
_____

Week Starting: _____

⑪

My Top 5 for this Week

Top 1 Done

○ ☐ _____

○ ☐ _____

○ ☐ _____

○ ☐ _____

○ ☐ _____

Are these aligned with my Monthly Top 5?

Perfection steals momentum. Progress builds success.

My top 5 for today

Top 1 Done

○ ☐ _____

○ ☐ _____

○ ☐ _____

○ ☐ _____

○ ☐ _____

Are these aligned with my Weekly Top 5?

Start early, finish strong, repeat daily.

Date: _____ Day: _____   (1)

My top win today was: _____

Today I am grateful for: _____

My top 5 for today

Top 1 Done

○ ☐ _____

○ ☐ _____

○ ☐ _____

○ ☐ _____

○ ☐ _____

Are these aligned with my Weekly Top 5?

Plant the seeds of success in the present
to harvest fulfillment later.

Date: _____ Day: _____ (2)

My top win today was: _____

Today I am grateful for: _____

My top 5 for today

Top 1   Done

○ ☐ _____

○ ☐ _____

○ ☐ _____

○ ☐ _____

○ ☐ _____

Are these aligned with my Weekly Top 5?

Start now and watch your confidence grow.

Date: _____ Day: _____   (3)

My top win today was: _____

Today I am grateful for: _____

My top 5 for today

Top 1 Done

○ ☐ _____

○ ☐ _____

○ ☐ _____

○ ☐ _____

○ ☐ _____

Are these aligned with my Weekly Top 5?

Simplicity isn't just minimalism
—it's clarity in action.

Date: _____ Day: _____ (4)

My top win today was: _____

Today I am grateful for: _____

My top 5 for today

Top 1 Done
○ □ _____

○ □ _____

○ □ _____

○ □ _____

○ □ _____

Are these aligned with my Weekly Top 5?

Every step forward is progress; every wait for perfect is wasted.

Date: _____ Day: _____ (5)

My top win today was: _____

Today I am grateful for: _____

My top 5 for today

Top 1   Done

○ ☐ _____

○ ☐ _____

○ ☐ _____

○ ☐ _____

○ ☐ _____

Are these aligned with my Weekly Top 5?

Speak kindly to yourself, and watch your confidence blossom.

Date: _____   Day: _____   (6)

My top win today was: _____

Today I am grateful for: _____

My top 5 for today

Top 1 Done

○ ☐ ....

○ ☐ ....

○ ☐ ....

○ ☐ ....

○ ☐ ....

Are these aligned with my Weekly Top 5?

Tackle tasks like opportunities,
not obligations.

Date: _____   Day: _____   (7)

My top win today was: _____

Today I am grateful for: _____

Week Ending: _____

My Week in Review

My top win this week was:

_____
_____
_____

I am grateful for:

_____
_____
_____

What could be improved or learned:

_____
_____
_____

Week Starting: _____

My Top 5 for this Week

Top 1 Done

O ☐ _____

O ☐ _____

O ☐ _____

O ☐ _____

O ☐ _____

Are these aligned with my Monthly Top 5?

Own the week—start strong, finish stronger.

My top 5 for today

Top 1   Done
○ □ _____

○ □ _____

○ □ _____

○ □ _____

○ □ _____

Are these aligned with my Weekly Top 5?

Prioritize what you truly want, or you'll forever chase distractions.

Date: _____ Day: _____ (8)

My top win today was:

Today I am grateful for:

My top 5 for today

Top 1 Done

◯ ☐ _____

◯ ☐ _____

◯ ☐ _____

◯ ☐ _____

◯ ☐ _____

Are these aligned with my Weekly Top 5?

Productive people plan,
then execute ruthlessly.

Date: _____ Day: _____ (9)

My top win today was: _____

Today I am grateful for: _____

My top 5 for today

Top 1　Done

○ ☐ _____

○ ☐ _____

○ ☐ _____

○ ☐ _____

○ ☐ _____

Are these aligned with my Weekly Top 5?

Procrastination won't pay your bills; action will.

Date: _____   Day: _____   (10)

My top win today was: _____

Today I am grateful for: _____

My top 5 for today

Top 1   Done

○ ☐ _____

○ ☐ _____

○ ☐ _____

○ ☐ _____

○ ☐ _____

Are these aligned with my Weekly Top 5?

Skip the small talk
—jump straight to the hustle.

Date: _____   Day: _____   (11)

My top win today was: _____

Today I am grateful for: _____

My top 5 for today

Top 1 Done

◯ ☐ _____

◯ ☐ _____

◯ ☐ _____

◯ ☐ _____

◯ ☐ _____

Are these aligned with my Weekly Top 5?

Procrastination only delays your greatness—act now.

Date: _____ Day: _____ (12)

My top win today was: _____

Today I am grateful for: _____

My top 5 for today

Top 1   Done

○ □ _____

○ □ _____

○ □ _____

○ □ _____

○ □ _____

Are these aligned with my Weekly Top 5?

Let the lack of support remind you that you're stronger than you thought.

Date: _____ Day: _____ (13)

My top win today was:

Today I am grateful for:

My top 5 for today

Top 1 Done

○ □ _____

○ □ _____

○ □ _____

○ □ _____

○ □ _____

Are these aligned with my Weekly Top 5?

Effort creates motivation; waiting simply wastes potential.

Date: _____ Day: _____ (14)

My top win today was:

Today I am grateful for:

Week Ending: _____

My Week in Review

My top win this week was:

_____
_____
_____

I am grateful for:

_____
_____
_____

What could be improved or learned:

_____
_____
_____

Week Starting: _____

My Top 5 for this Week

Top 1 Done
○ ☐ _____

○ ☐ _____

○ ☐ _____

○ ☐ _____

○ ☐ _____

Are these aligned with my Monthly Top 5?

Every day is a step forward—stack them wisely.

My top 5 for today

Top 1   Done
○ ☐ _____

○ ☐ _____

○ ☐ _____

○ ☐ _____

○ ☐ _____

Are these aligned with my Weekly Top 5?

Let your courage be louder than your fear of failure.

Date: _____ Day: _____ (15)

My top win today was: _____

Today I am grateful for: _____

My top 5 for today

Top 1 Done

○ ☐ _____

○ ☐ _____

○ ☐ _____

○ ☐ _____

○ ☐ _____

Are these aligned with my Weekly Top 5?

Perfection starves success; progress feeds it daily.

Date: _____ Day: _____ (16)

My top win today was: _____

Today I am grateful for: _____

My top 5 for today

Top 1 Done

○ ☐ _____

○ ☐ _____

○ ☐ _____

○ ☐ _____

○ ☐ _____

Are these aligned with my Weekly Top 5?

Perfection sleeps on dreams;
progress awakens them.

Date: _____ Day: _____ (17)

My top win today was: _____

Today I am grateful for: _____

My top 5 for today

Top 1 Done

○ ☐ _____

○ ☐ _____

○ ☐ _____

○ ☐ _____

○ ☐ _____

Are these aligned with my Weekly Top 5?

Let your first thought in the morning be one of thanks—it sets the tone for the day.

Date: _____ Day: _____ (18)

My top win today was:

Today I am grateful for:

My top 5 for today

Top 1   Done

◯ ☐ _____

◯ ☐ _____

◯ ☐ _____

◯ ☐ _____

◯ ☐ _____

Are these aligned with my Weekly Top 5?

Let your list hold your tasks so your mind can focus on solutions.

Date: _____ Day: _____   (19)

My top win today was: _____

Today I am grateful for: _____

My top 5 for today

Top 1　Done

○ ☐ _____

○ ☐ _____

○ ☐ _____

○ ☐ _____

○ ☐ _____

Are these aligned with my Weekly Top 5?

Perfection is an endless wait;
progress happens now.

Date: _____ Day: _____ (20)

My top win today was: _____

Today I am grateful for: _____

My top 5 for today

Top 1   Done

○ ☐ _____

○ ☐ _____

○ ☐ _____

○ ☐ _____

○ ☐ _____

Are these aligned with my Weekly Top 5?

Let your spirit sing louder
than your doubts.

Date: _____   Day: _____   (21)

My top win today was: _____

Today I am grateful for: _____

Week Ending: _____

(13)

My Week in Review

My top win this week was:

_____
_____

I am grateful for:

_____
_____

What could be improved or learned:

_____
_____

Week Starting: _____

My Top 5 for this Week

Top 1 Done

○ ☐ _____

○ ☐ _____

○ ☐ _____

○ ☐ _____

○ ☐ _____

Are these aligned with my Monthly Top 5?

Win the morning, win the week.

My top 5 for today

Top 1 Done

○ ☐ _____

○ ☐ _____

○ ☐ _____

○ ☐ _____

○ ☐ _____

Are these aligned with my Weekly Top 5?

Perfection is stalling;
progress is creating.

Date: _____ Day: _____ (22)

My top win today was: _____

Today I am grateful for: _____

My top 5 for today

Top 1 Done

○ ☐ _____

○ ☐ _____

○ ☐ _____

○ ☐ _____

○ ☐ _____

Are these aligned with my Weekly Top 5?

Perfection is the enemy of momentum;
progress fuels your journey.

Date: _____ Day: _____ (23)

My top win today was: _____

Today I am grateful for: _____

My top 5 for today

Top 1   Done

○ ☐ _____

○ ☐ _____

○ ☐ _____

○ ☐ _____

○ ☐ _____

Are these aligned with my Weekly Top 5?

Let your work be the story you tell,
not just your words.

Date: _____ Day: _____ (24)

_____
_____
_____
_____
_____
_____
_____
_____
_____
_____
_____
_____
_____
_____
_____
_____
_____
_____
_____
_____
_____
_____
_____
_____
_____

My top win today was: _____

Today I am grateful for: _____

My top 5 for today

Top 1 Done

○ □ _____

○ □ _____

○ □ _____

○ □ _____

○ □ _____

Are these aligned with my Weekly Top 5?

Liberate your mind by storing ideas in a trusted system.

Date: _____ Day: _____ (25)

My top win today was: _____

Today I am grateful for: _____

My top 5 for today

Top 1 Done
○ ☐ _____

○ ☐ _____

○ ☐ _____

○ ☐ _____

○ ☐ _____

Are these aligned with my Weekly Top 5?

Perfection is tomorrow's excuse;
progress is today's triumph.

Date: _____ Day: _____ (26)

My top win today was: _____

Today I am grateful for: _____

My top 5 for today

Top 1 Done

○ ☐ _____

○ ☐ _____

○ ☐ _____

○ ☐ _____

○ ☐ _____

Are these aligned with my Weekly Top 5?

Life rewards those who chase it, not those who wait for it.

Date: _____   Day: _____   (27)

My top win today was: _____

Today I am grateful for: _____

My top 5 for today

Top 1 Done

○ □ _____

○ □ _____

○ □ _____

○ □ _____

○ □ _____

Are these aligned with my Weekly Top 5?

Perfection is too heavy a burden;
progress lifts you step by step.

Date: _____ Day: _____   (28)

My top win today was: _____

Today I am grateful for: _____

Week Ending: _____ (14)

My Week in Review

My top win this week was:

_____
_____
_____

I am grateful for:

_____
_____
_____

What could be improved or learned:

_____
_____
_____

Week Starting: _____

My Top 5 for this Week

Top 1 Done

○ ☐ _____

○ ☐ _____

○ ☐ _____

○ ☐ _____

○ ☐ _____

Are these aligned with my Monthly Top 5?

A productive week starts with a single focused task.

My top 5 for today

Top 1   Done

○ ☐ _____

○ ☐ _____

○ ☐ _____

○ ☐ _____

○ ☐ _____

Are these aligned with my Weekly Top 5?

Perfection keeps score; progress celebrates effort.

Date: _____   Day: _____   (29)

My top win today was: _____

Today I am grateful for: _____

My top 5 for today

Top 1 Done

○ ☐ _____

○ ☐ _____

○ ☐ _____

○ ☐ _____

○ ☐ _____

Are these aligned with my Weekly Top 5?

Let self-confidence be your superpower.

Date: _____ Day: _____ (30)

My top win today was: _____

Today I am grateful for: _____

My top 5 for today

Top 1 Done

○ ☐ _____

○ ☐ _____

○ ☐ _____

○ ☐ _____

○ ☐ _____

Are these aligned with my Weekly Top 5?

Life sparkles more when you acknowledge every gift, big or small.

Date: _____ Day: _____   (31)

My top win today was: _____

Today I am grateful for: _____

Quarter: _____ to _____

My 3 Big Priorities This Quarter

Priority 1:

_____

_____

Priority 2:

_____

_____

Priority 3:

_____

_____

How Did I Go on My Big 3?

Priority 1:

_____

_____

Priority 2:

_____

_____

Priority 3:

_____

_____

Notes

Perfection is a thief.

SAM PENNY
The Topify Method

topifymethod.com

www.ingramcontent.com/pod-product-compliance
Lightning Source LLC
Chambersburg PA
CBHW072150200426
43209CB00052B/1102